BEFORE
YOUR
BIRTH DAY

WHAT PEOPLE ARE SAYING ...

As an obstetrician and a father of four, I know that for many children, their birth marks the beginning of time. This beautifully written and illustrated children's book shows children their story before they were born, the story leading up to their birth. Expertly written and illustrated with multicultural families, this is a book that every parent will enjoy sharing with their children.
–Allan T. Sawyer, MD, Obstetrician/Gynecologist, Peoria, Arizona

This book is a wonderful story of poetry, starting from the decision for a new life, through the development and birth of a true gift from God. The illustrations beautifully show the marvel of fetal development. Well done!
–Michael A. Urig MD, Obstetrician/Gynecologist, Phoenix, Arizona

I love the way this book tells the story of the journey a baby takes before birth. This process is explained in a simple, clear way that makes it easy to understand. The illustrations are simply beautiful and really capture a baby's journey in utero, explaining the growth and development at various stages of pregnancy. This book is a must read and portrays the beauty and miraculous journey of God's most precious gift!
–Shawna Marr, RN, BSN, Certified OB-RN

Before Your Birth Day is heartwarming. The simplicity and colorful illustrations create a beautiful way for parents to help young children understand the miracle of life.
–Mary Hubenthal, RN, BSN

BEFORE YOUR BIRTH DAY

Teresa Joyelle Krager
illustrated by Thalita Dol

PUBLISHING THE POSITIVE

ELK LAKE PUBLISHING INC
Plymouth, Massachusetts

Cover Design: Thalita Dol, Derinda Babcock

Interior Design: Derinda Babcock

Editor(s): Derinda Babcock, Deb Haggerty

Illustrated by: Thalita Dol

Published by: Elk Lake Publishing, Inc., Plymouth, Massachusetts 02360

Library Cataloging Data

Names: Krager, Teresa (Teresa Krager)

Before Your Birth Day / Teresa Krager

46 p., 21.6 cm × 21.6 cm (8.5 in. × 8.5 in.)

Identifiers: ISBN-13: 978-1-64949-011-7 (paperback) | 978-1-64949-012-4 (trade hardcover) | 978-1-64949-013-1 (trade paperback) | 978-1-64949-014-8 (e-book)

Key Words: Children ages 4 to 8, Birthday, Stages of development, Family relationships, Curiosities and Wonders, New Baby, Pregnancy

LCCN: 2020940684 Nonfiction

AUTHOR'S DEDICATION

For the Lord and for Gideon.

For all the babies whose lives here were much too brief.

ILLUSTRATOR'S DEDICATION

For my baby Toni,

who didn't get to finish this incredible journey on earth.

For Jesus, my comfort.

Before your *birth* day,
Before you were born,
Before all the presents
With wrapping all torn ...

1

Yes, *before* your birth day,
God made plans for you.
Part of Mom, part of Dad,
He blended the two.

2

3

God saw you and shaped you,
A wonderful sight.
You, in Mom's safe place,
Heaven's delight.

5 weeks

Soon Mommy found out
You were growing inside.
An apple seed size,
You could easily hide.

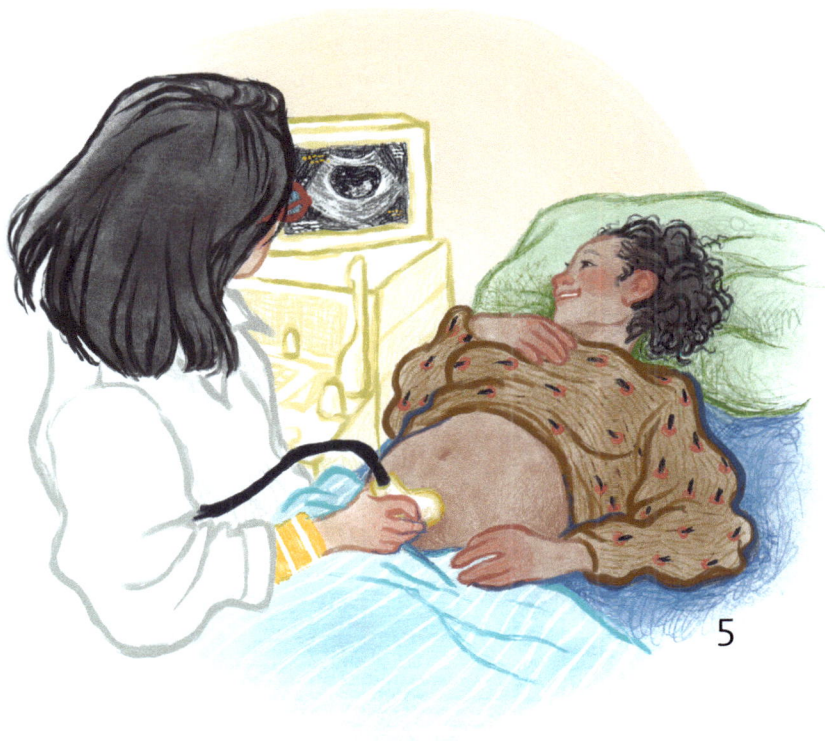

Bigger by six weeks,
An orange seed size.
Your skin was see-through.

6

Your heart beat.

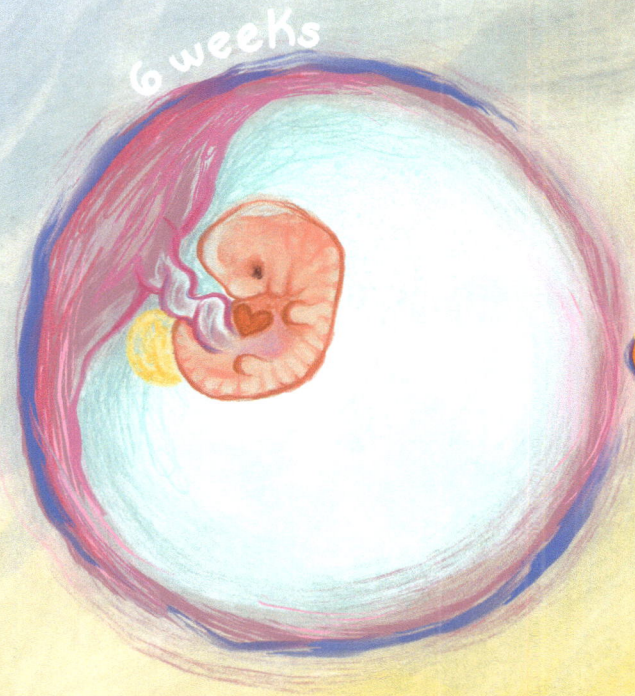

6 weeks

Surprise!

That sound was amazing,
A swooshing woo-hoo.
The doctor could hear it,
The miracle of *you*,
A whispering, swooshing of woo-hoo, woo-hoo.

7

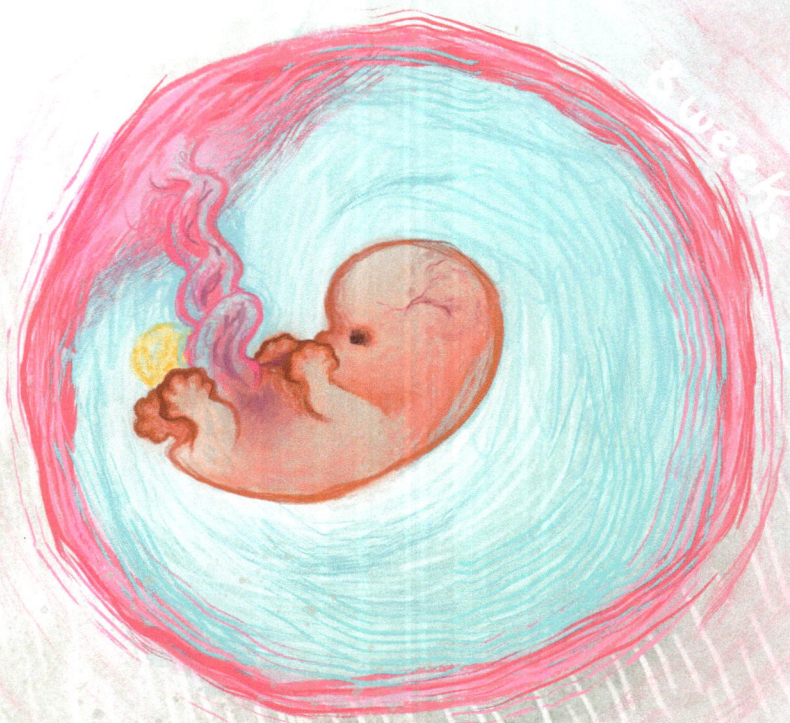

Your new brain was forming
And spinal cord too.
Their job? Tell your small body
Just what to do.

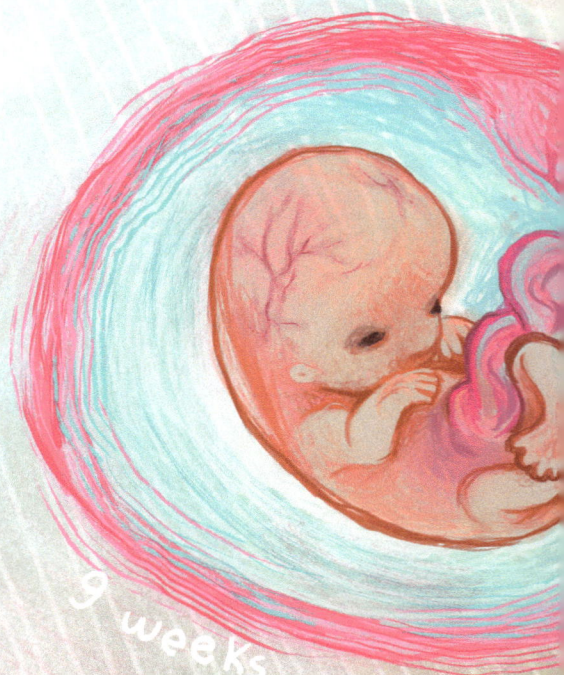

8

5 weeks

9 weeks

Now, the size of a grape,
Arms and legs s-t-r-e-t-c-h-e-d to grow.
At nine weeks of life,
Your face started to show.

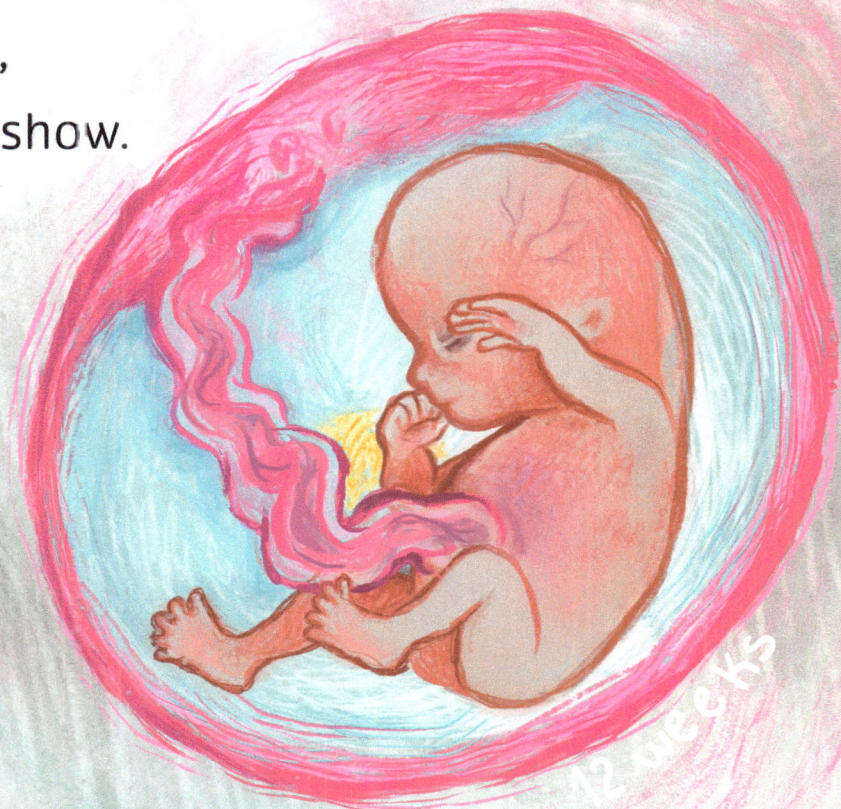

Next, you grew fingernails.
Wiggled your toes.
At twelve weeks along,
Hands could open and close.

9

Then, eyes and ears moved
S-l-o-w-l-y into their place.
Were you making faces
Inside that small space?

Weeks fifteen through eighteen

Your head grew fine hair.

Muscles got stronger,

You kicked here and there.

18 weeks

Twenty weeks of living
In Mom, half-way done.
Stronger bones. Longer legs.
A granddaughter or son?

A banana size now,
Twenty-one weeks along.
You heard Mommy's voice
When she sang you a song,
A hummin' and drummin' and strum sing-along.

You hiccupped and swallowed
The water around you,
Practice for breathing when
Air would surround you.

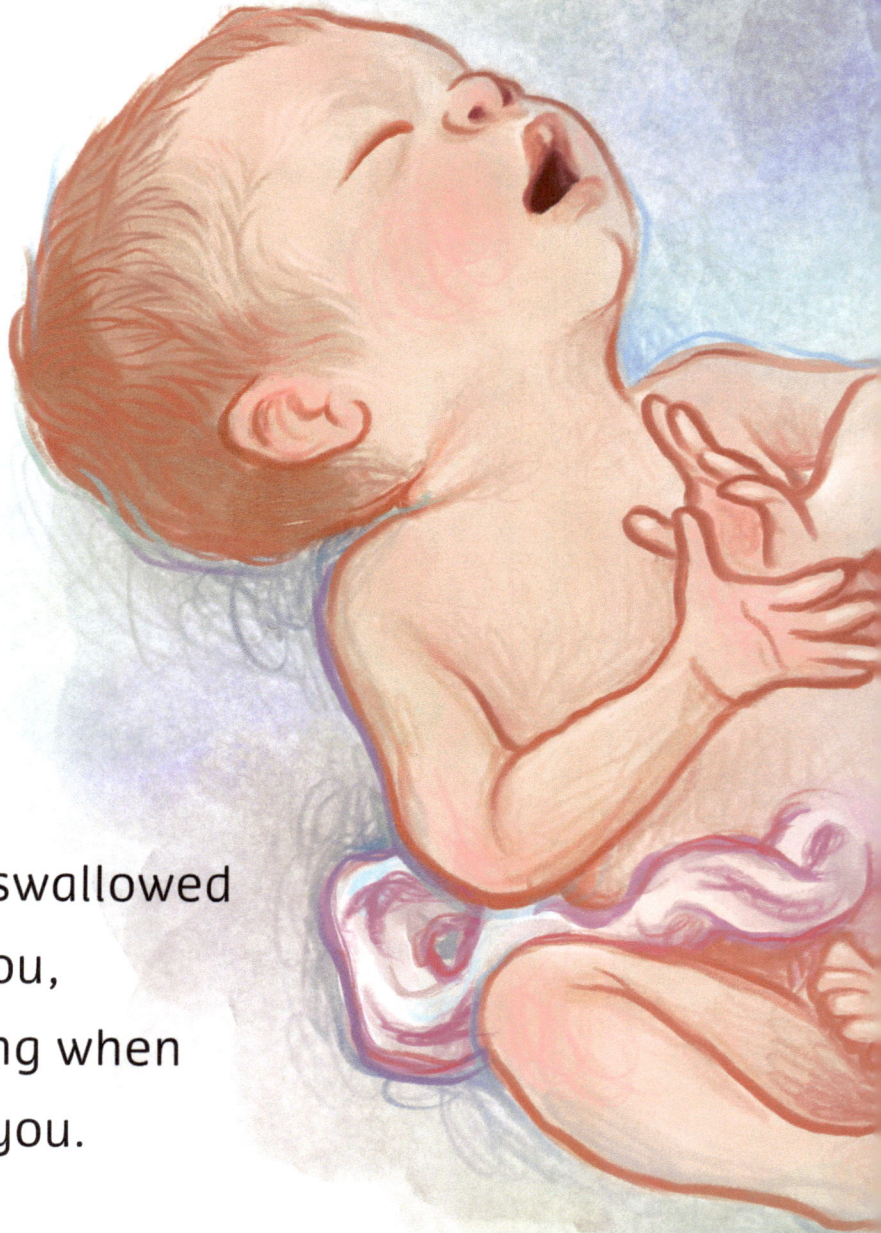

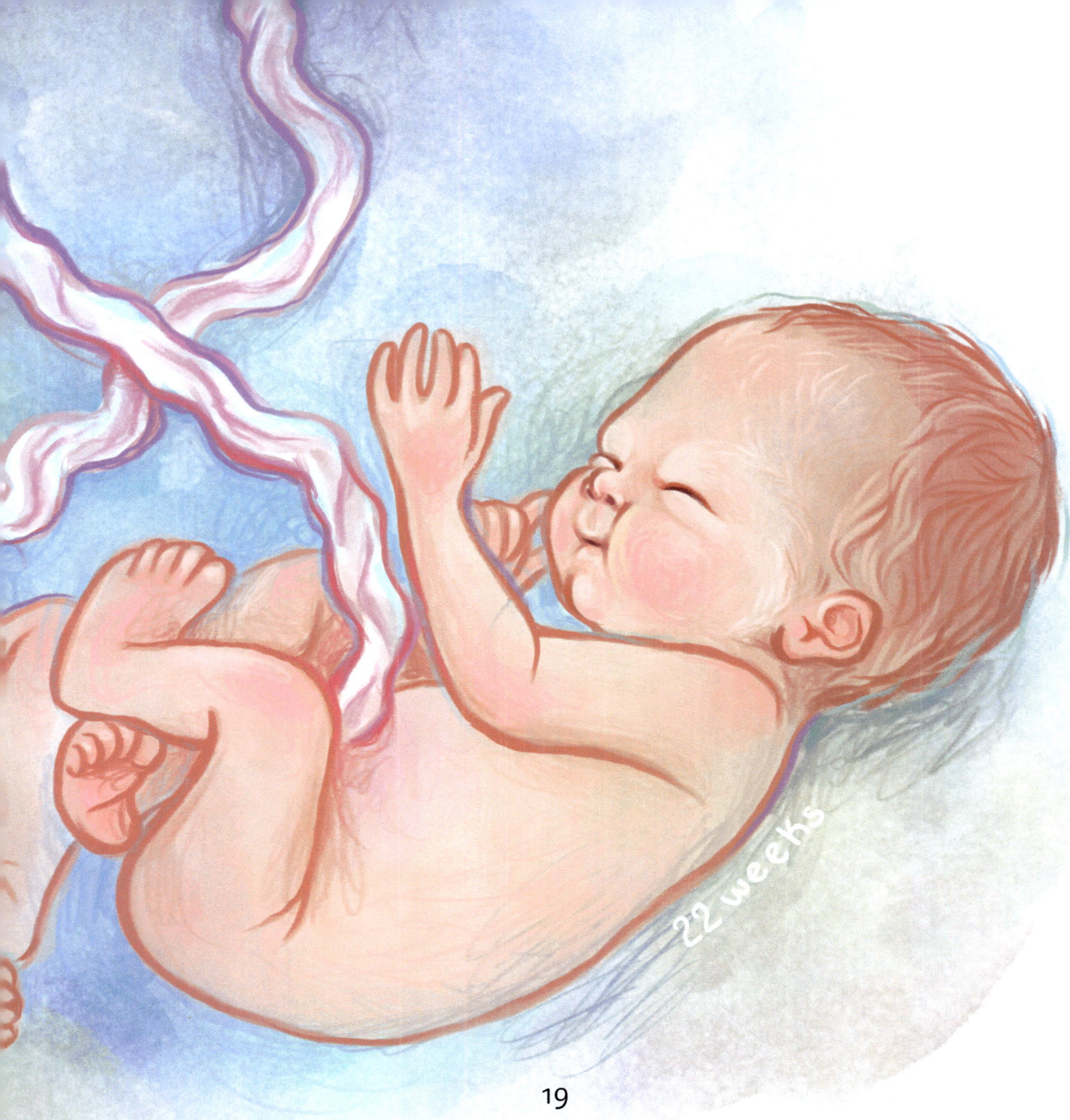

22 weeks

19

20

Eyebrows and eyelashes,
God watched them grow.
They'll come in handy
For keeping out snow.

Footprints and fingerprints,
None just like yours,
One day will show up
On fridge, windows, and doors.

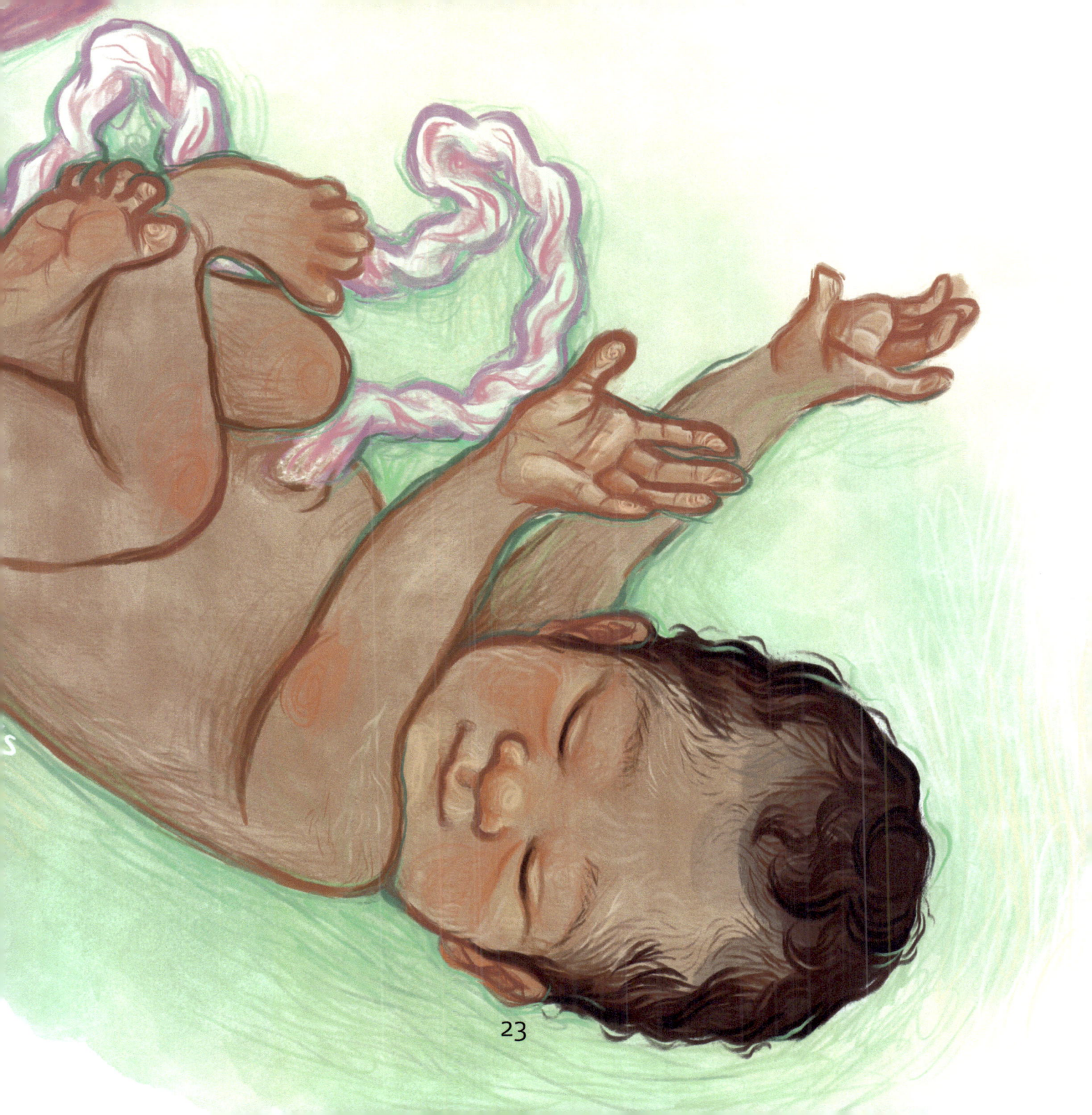

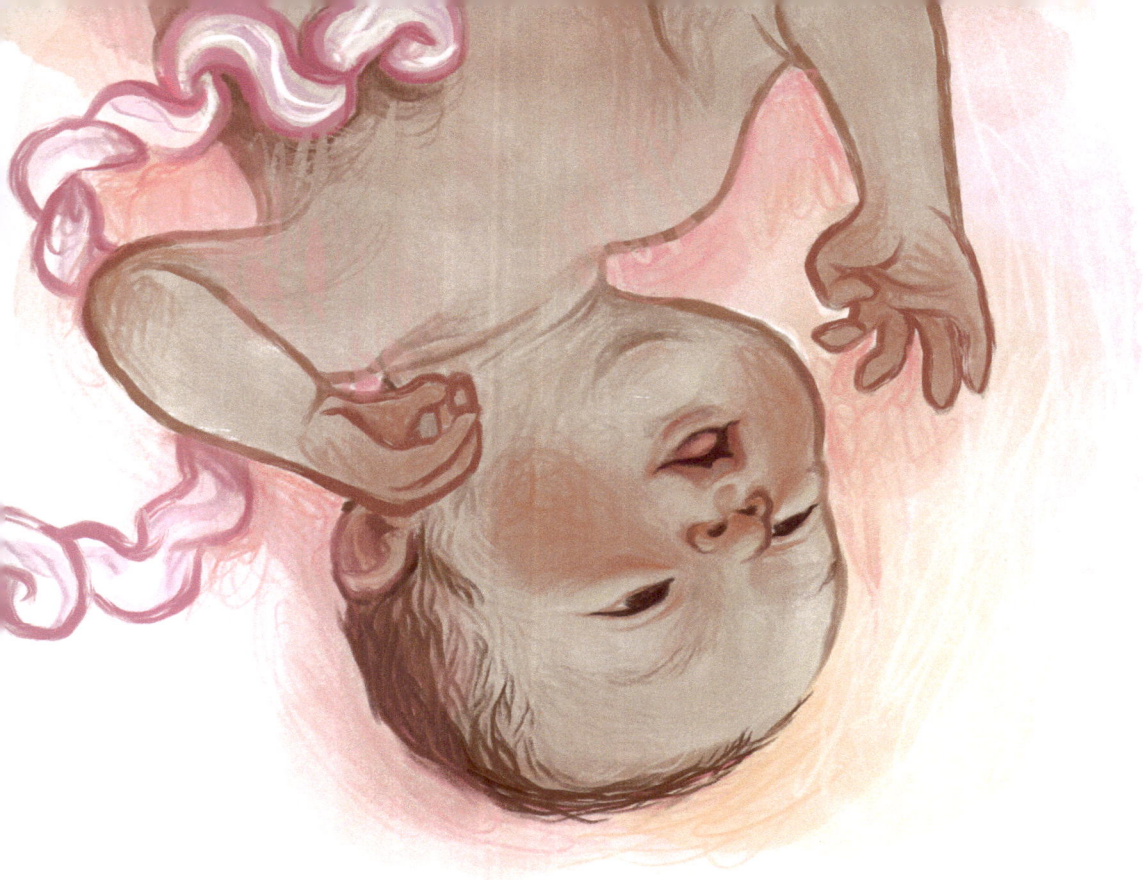

Weighing two pounds
By your twenty-eighth week,

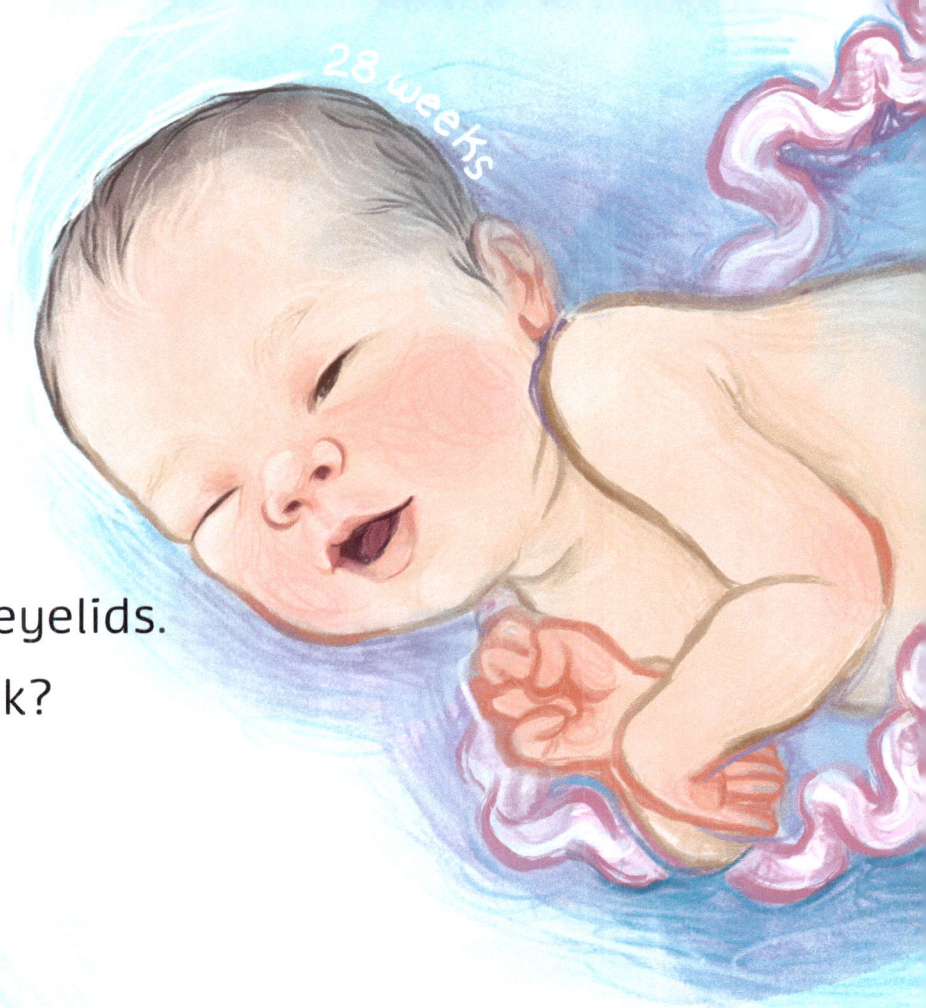

You opened your eyelids.

Did you try to peek?

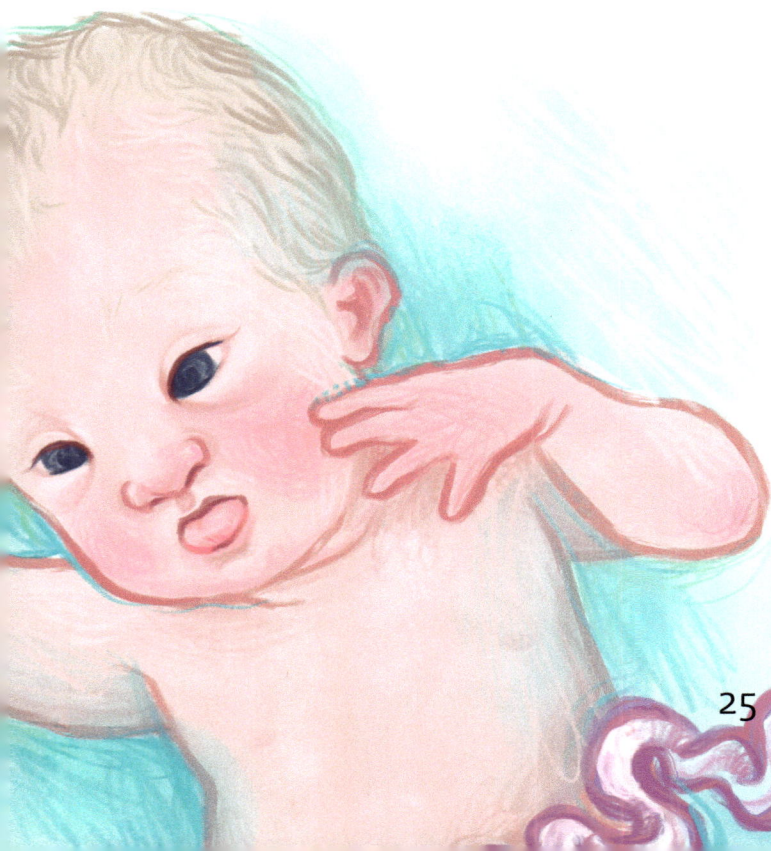

28 weeks

25

32 weeks

26

Your senses got better.
Smell that and taste this.
You touched your own face
Grammy waited to kiss!

27

Another few weeks,

And your eyes could see light

Right through Mommy's tummy,

Her skin stretching tight.

36 weeks

30

A layer of fat
For your soft, wrinkly skin.
Will you have a dimple
When you flash a grin,
A chink in your cheeks or your chinny-chin-chin?

Weighing six pounds,
Maybe more, maybe less.
When *will* you be born?
We all try to guess.

January February March April May June July

August September October November December

33

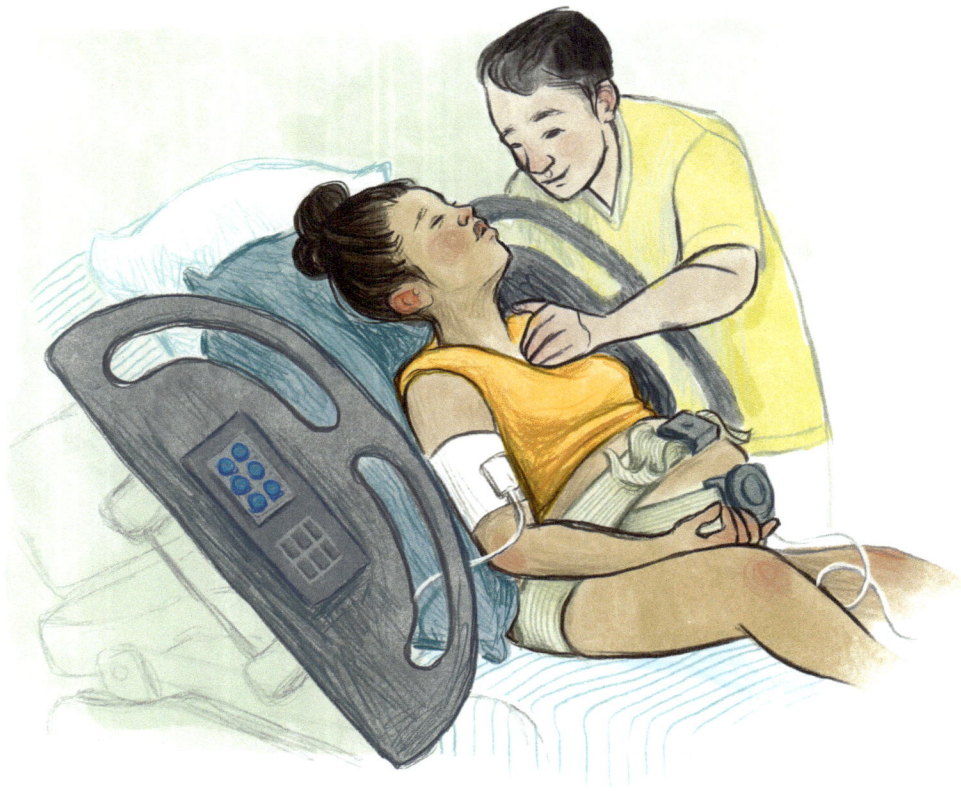

God sees all your days.
He knows when and how,
But Mommy and Daddy
Are ready right *now*.

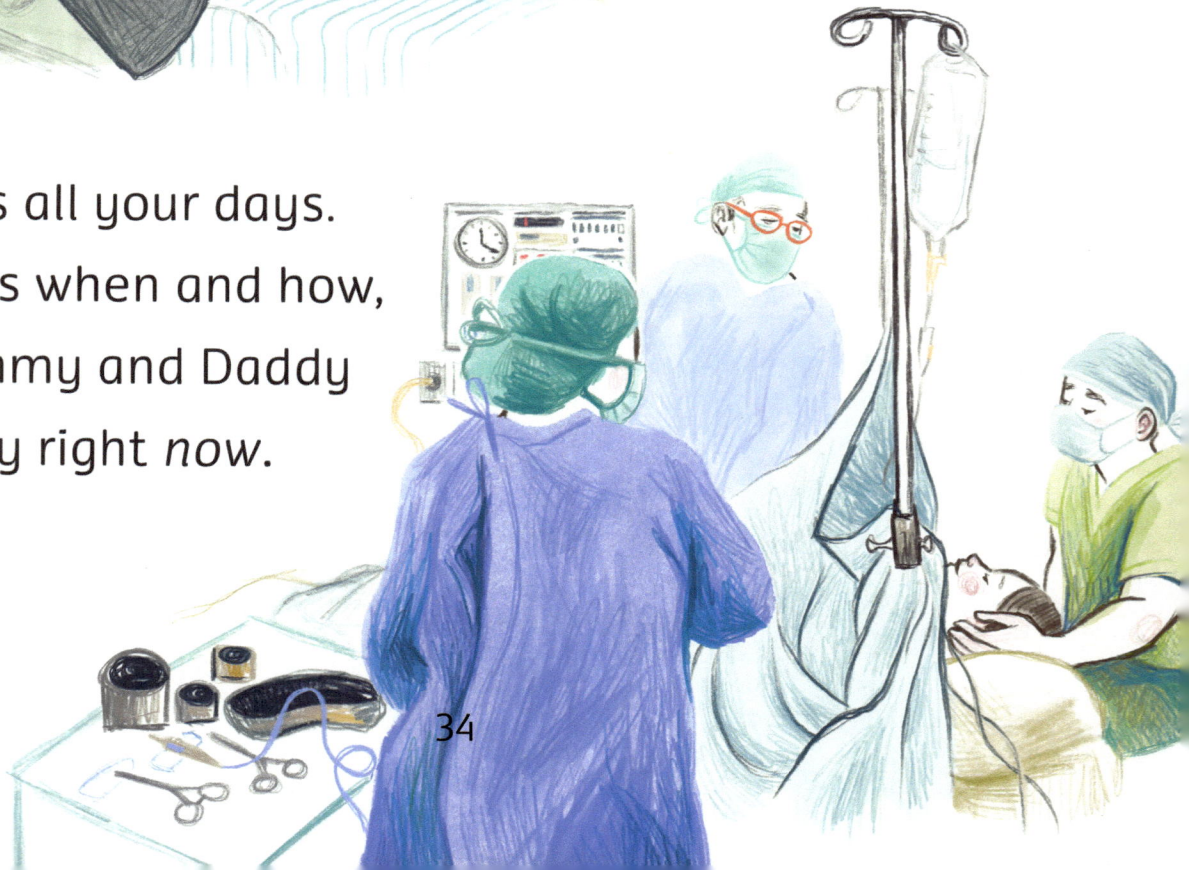

34

35

Then finally ... your *birth* day!

Let's have a parade

To celebrate *you*,
God so wonderfully made!

Teresa J. Krager

With a master's in education
Taught twenty-seven years,
K and first grade dedication.
With Seuss in her head
And a Spirit of inspiration,
Brings God's Word to life
For picture book creation.

Teresa lives with her husband
In a desert location.
Five kids and five grandkids
Bring much celebration.
Loving music, songwriting,
And a snowboard vacation,
She's now thrilled to offer
Her debut presentation:

Before Your Birth Day

www.teresakrager.com

www.pointingtheway.live

Thalita Dol

Is always creating.

She loves drawing, sewing,

And even decorating.

She grew up in Rio

Where the sun's always high,

But now lives in Vancouver.

She loves it, that's why.

At home with her husband

And two daughters of their own,

There is always adventure.

She is never alone.

www.thalitadol.com

@thalitadolillustration